Discover It Yourself

Sound
and Light

KINGFISHER
LONDON & NEW YORK

KINGFISHER
LONDON & NEW YORK

Published 2020 by Kingfisher
Published in the United States by
Kingfisher, 120 Broadway,
New York, NY 10271
Kingfisher is an imprint of
Macmillan Children's Books,
London
Copyright © Macmillan Publishers
International Ltd. 1995, 2020

Designed by Tall Tree
Illustrated by Diego Vaisberg/
Advocate Art

ISBN 978-0-7534-7686-4 (HB)
978-0-7534-7688-8 (PB)

First published in 1995 by
Kingfisher
This fully revised and updated
edition published
2020 by Kingfisher

Library of Congress Cataloging-in-
Publication data has been
applied for.

Kingfisher books are available for
special promotions and
premiums. For details contact:
Special Markets Department,
Macmillan, 120 Broadway, New
York, NY 1027

Printed in China
9 8 7 6 5 4 3 2 1
1TR/1120/WKT/UG/128MA

Contents

Make sure you have a grown-up to help whenever you see this sign.

!

Thunder and Lightning

Have you ever been caught in a thunderstorm? First you see a flash of lightning, then you hear a crash of thunder. The sky is filled with light and sound. Lightning flashes are huge sparks of electricity. They are so powerful that they can be seen a long way from a storm. Light travels very fast, so we see the flash of light in the same second that it is made. But sound travels more slowly. It may be several seconds before the sound of a thunderclap reaches our ears.

The Vikings believed that thunder was the sound of their god Odin hammering his sword ready for war.

How Far Is the Storm?

Light travels a million times faster than sound, so it arrives almost instantly. But sound takes about 5 seconds to travel 1 mile. You can figure out how far a thunderstorm is from you by timing the number of seconds between seeing a lightning flash and hearing the roll of thunder. If you count 2½ seconds, then the storm is half a mile away; 5 seconds means that it is 1 mile away; 10 seconds 2 miles; and so on.

Eye Spy

Look out for light arriving before you hear sound. For example, next time you go to a firework display, see if you can see the rockets exploding before you hear the bangs.

The giant sparks of electricity given off by lightning can strike tall trees and set them on fire. So never shelter under a tree during a thunderstorm.

In cities, many tall buildings have lightning rods running down their sides. These metal rods carry the electricity safely down the buildings into the ground.

Sound Waves

If you flick the end of a rope up and down, the "flick" travels along the rope like a wave—the section of rope in your hand passes the movement on to the next section, which passes it on again, and so on. This is how sound travels through the air. When you burst a balloon, the escaping air gives a sudden push to the air around it. This push is passed on through the air like the wave traveling along the rope, and we hear the loud bang, or pop, when the sound wave reaches our ears.

Making a Bang

Popping an air-filled paper bag forces the air trapped inside the bag through the hole in the paper. This sends a powerful sound wave through the air that reaches our ears as a loud bang.

Tie a rope to a tree or to a lamppost and flick the free end up and down to see how waves move along the rope.

Passing It On

Set up a row of dominoes, spacing them fairly close together. Now knock the first one over and watch how the wave travels down the line.

DISCOVER IT YOURSELF!

Build a sound cannon so you can see a sound wave make a candle flicker. You will need a cardboard tube, some plastic, scissors, tape, a small candle, a saucer, and some sand.

!

1. Stretch the pieces of plastic tightly across each end of the cardboard tube and tape them firmly in place.

2. Make a small hole in the middle of the plastic at one end of the tube.

3. Put some sand in the saucer and stand the candle upright in it. Ask an adult to light the candle for you.

4. Hold the end of the tube with the hole in it about an inch away from the flame.

5. Tap the other end of the tube with your finger. Watch what happens to the flame.

? How It Works

When you tap the plastic, you make a sound wave that travels down the tube and out of the hole at the end. The wave can be strong enough to blow out the candle flame.

7

Feeling Sound

If you bend the end of a ruler over the edge of a table and then let it go, the ruler will move up and down. When something moves quickly back and forth like this, we say that it is vibrating. Try changing the length of the ruler on the table. The shorter the length over the edge, the quicker the vibrations and the higher the sound. The number of sound waves a second is called the frequency of the waves. Almost every sound you hear is made by something vibrating.

Feeling Vibrations

When something is making a steady sound, it must be vibrating to push the air around it back and forth. If you hold your hand against things making sounds, you can usually feel the vibrations. Here are some things to test:
• a purring cat
• a ringing telephone
• your throat when you are singing
• a speaker playing loud music

Seeing Vibrations

We cannot see sound waves, but sometimes we can see the vibrations that make sounds. Sprinkle a few grains of uncooked rice on some paper, lay it over a radio or speaker, and watch the rice jump!

Press this end down firmly

If you stretch a rubber band between your fingers and twang it, it vibrates and makes a quiet sound. The sound isn't very loud because the band is small and it can only push a small amount of air. To make the sound louder, we must amplify it. In other words, we must make the vibrations of the elastic band push more air to and fro.

DISCOVER IT YOURSELF!

Make a sound amplifier. You will need a large plastic mixing bowl, a sheet of plastic cut from a plastic bag, tape, scissors, and two rubber bands.

1. Stretch the plastic tightly over the top of the bowl, like the skin of a drum. Secure the plastic with a rubber band and tape.

2. Tape the other rubber band to the middle of the plastic.

3. Now stretch the loose band and twang it.

? How It Works

When the band vibrates, it makes the stretched plastic vibrate. Because the plastic sheet is much bigger than the elastic band, it pushes a lot more air and amplifies the sound. That's why a jackhammer makes a very loud noise—it vibrates the ground around it.

Making Music

All musical instruments use vibrations to make sounds. Stringed instruments, like guitars and cellos, have stretched strings that vibrate when they are plucked, strummed, or bowed. Wind instruments, like flutes and clarinets, make vibrations when you blow into or across the mouthpiece. Percussion instruments, like drums and cymbals, are usually played by hitting or tapping them to make them vibrate.

Eye Spy

When you hear an orchestra or a band playing, see if you can pick out the sounds of different instruments.

Moving Air

Because a triangle moves only a small amount of air, it makes a quiet sound. The cymbals are bigger and move a lot more air. So they make a loud sound when they are crashed together.

The trumpet is a brass instrument. The player makes sounds by vibrating her lips.

10

DISCOVER IT YOURSELF!

Make your own musical instruments.

1. Make a trumpet with a short piece of hose and a funnel. When you blow into it, try to vibrate your lips—it takes a lot of practice to get a clear note.

2. Try blowing over the top of an empty bottle. If you fill several bottles with different amounts of water, you can get high and low notes. Or you could blow sharply over a pen lid to make a high, piercing whistle.

3. Make a rich, deep note with a string bass like the one in the picture. Ask an adult to drill a hole in one end of the pole so you can thread string through it. Knot the string tightly under the top of the box and pluck it. Cut a large hole in the box to make the sound louder.

4. Tap small cans, large pans, big, empty boxes, or glass jars with pens, spoons, or anything else you can find. Some things will make dull sounds that fade quickly. Others vibrate for longer and make bright sounds that ring on.

Your Own Band

Ask your friends to make musical instruments, too. Then you can start your own band.

Moving Sound

Sound can travel through other things besides air. Test this out by asking a friend to tap some metal railings with a stick while you stand farther down the railings. You should be able to hear the sound, but if you put your ear close to the metal, the sound will be a lot louder. Sound also travels well through water. In fact, sound travels five times faster through water than it does through air.

Eye Spy

Next time you swim in a pool or the ocean, listen to how different everything sounds underwater. (Only try this if you can swim really well!)

!

DISCOVER IT YOURSELF!

Make a yogurt container telephone to hear sounds travel along string.

1. Ask an adult to help you make a small hole in the bottom of each container.

2. Thread the ends of the string through each hole and knot them. Hold one of the containers to your ear while a friend speaks into the other. Remember to keep the string tightly stretched.

? How It Works

Your friend's voice makes the bottom of his or her container vibrate. This make the string vibrate, too. The sound waves travel along the string, making the bottom of your container vibrate so that you hear your friend's voice.

Bouncing Sound

If you shout when you are standing in a tunnel or in a large, empty room, the sound made by your voice will hit the walls and bounce back. This reflected sound is called an echo. Echoes are louder when they hit a hard barrier, like the walls of a tunnel. Soft materials, like carpets and drapes, absorb or soak up sound. That's why you will hear an echo in an empty room but will not in one that is full of furniture.

Animal Echoes

Bats find food by making high-pitched squeaks and then listening for the echoes from insects. Dolphins use echoes to find food, too.

Making Echoes

Good places to experiment with echoes are near high cliffs or under bridges. If you face a cliff and shout loudly, the sound waves will hit the hard rock and bounce back. You may even hear several echoes if the sound is reflected from different parts of the cliff. Echoes made under bridges are louder than ones made by a cliff because the sounds have no room to spread out.

DISCOVER IT YOURSELF!

Test different materials to find out which ones are better at reflecting sound.

1. Set up the experiment as shown, making sure that the cardboard tubes do not touch and that they are about 2 inches from the material to be tested.

2. Move the listening tube from left to right until you catch the sound of the clock's tick.

3. Try listening for the reflected sound against the wall first. Then you could try paper, cloth, a metal tray, a mirror, and a cushion. Which materials reflect the sound best? Which absorb it?

Paper

Metal

Cloth

? How It Works

The strongest reflection comes from hard, smooth materials like metal or glass. The sound bounces off the materials at the same angle that it strikes—like a ball bouncing off a smooth floor.

You will hear the loudest sound when the tube is at the correct angle to catch the reflection.

How Do You Hear?

The drawing below shows what the inside of your ear looks like. The part outside your head catches sounds. Inside, there is a small piece of skin stretched tight like the skin on a drum. This is called the eardrum. When sounds enter your ear, they make the eardrum vibrate. The vibrations are amplified and are picked up by nerves. The nerves then send signals about the sound to your brain and you "hear."

Hearing Aids

Hearing aids help people who can't hear very well. They are tiny electrical amplifiers that pick up and amplify sounds as they enter the ear.

Nerves

Eardrum

How Loud Is Loud?

The loudness of a sound is measured in decibels (dB for short). Sounds over 100 dB can damage your ears.

- Airplane 100–150 dB
- Jackhammer 100 dB
- Loud music 90–95 dB
- Talking 40–60 dB
- Whispering 20 dB
- Falling leaves 10 dB

WARNING!

(!) Never push anything into your ear. If you burst your eardrum, you may become deaf.

DISCOVER IT YOURSELF!

Can you tell which direction sounds are coming from?

1. Put on a blindfold and ask a friend to make a sound, sometimes from behind you and sometimes to the right or left.

2. Try pointing in the direction of the sound each time. You could experiment with different sounds (like humming) and distances.

3. Try blocking one ear. Does this make it easier or more difficult to tell the direction of the sound?

Eye Spy

Watch for animals using their ears. Hares can twist their long ears around so they can check where a sound is coming from. Sometimes you can see birds tilting their heads toward sounds, too.

Light Waves

Without light from the Sun, Earth would be a dark, cold, lifeless place. Light is a kind of energy. We use light to see. Plants use it to grow. Like sound, light travels in waves. But light does not need to travel through air or water. It can pass through empty space where there is no air or water to carry it. Light waves travel in straight lines, but they travel so fast that we can't see them move. We just see a straight, steady beam of light.

First Light Bulb

The first electric light was invented by Thomas Edison in 1879. He used electricity to heat a piece of burned thread so that it glowed brightly.

Light All Around

We need light to be able to see. During the day, we get light from the Sun. At night, or in a dark room, we use artificial light, such as light from electric light bulbs. When you read a book by sunlight or by lamp light, the light is reflected from the pages of the book into your eyes. Different things reflect different amounts of light. That is why some things look shiny and bright and others look dull.

See for yourself how light travels in straight lines. You will need a bright flashlight and some cardboard.

1. Cut out three pieces of cardboard the same size and make a small hole in the center of each of them.

2. Line up the cardboard pieces so you can see the light shining through the holes. (You could support them in modeling clay or ask a friend to help.)

3. Now move the middle card from side to side. You will only be able to see the light when the three holes are in a straight line.

Straight Beams

Sometimes, rays of sunlight are broken up by trees or clouds. You can then see that the light rays are straight.

Never look directly at the Sun or a bright light.

19

Light and Shade

Some things, like glass and water, are transparent. This means that light can pass through them. Other things, like metal and stone, are opaque. They block out the light. Because light travels in straight lines, it cannot bend around opaque objects, so these things cast shadows. The middle part of a shadow is very dark. It is called the umbra. The lighter edge is called the penumbra.

Light passes through the transparent glass of the window, so we can see through it. But the shade is opaque and blocks out the Sun's light.

DISCOVER IT YOURSELF!

See how shadows work.

Put a piece of white paper on a table under a bright lamp. Hold a small piece of thick cardboard or a coaster in front of the light to make a shadow. Try moving the cardboard toward and away from the light to see how the shadow's shape changes.

Fly's Eye View

If a fly sat in the middle of the umbra, it would see a dark circle blocking out the light. A fly on the penumbra would see part of the light shining past the cardboard.

Note: A fly doesn't really see like us! Take a look at page 29

Shadows in Space

Total eclipse—
as seen from
the umbra

Partial eclipse—
as seen from the
penumbra

When the Moon passes between the Sun and Earth, it blocks out the Sun's light and casts a shadow on Earth. This is called an eclipse of the Sun. Where the middle of the Moon's shadow (the umbra) falls on Earth, there is a total eclipse of the Sun. Where the edge of its shadow falls on Earth, there is a partial eclipse of the Sun.

DISCOVER IT YOURSELF!

Your own body is opaque—that's why you have a shadow. Why not set up a shadow screen and play some shadow games.

Use a good, bright light, such as a slide projector. Hang up a white sheet for your screen. Stand close to the sheet to cast a dark, clear shadow.

Things to Try

- Guess an object from its shadow's shape.
- Draw around shadows made by people's faces to make silhouettes.
- Make shadow puppets and put on a play.

21

Look in the Mirror

When light hits a surface, the light rays are reflected, or bounced back. Flat, shiny surfaces reflect light best. That's why mirrors are made of flat, highly polished glass with a shiny silver coating on the back. When you look in a mirror, you can see a reflection of yourself. Mirrors can be used to change the direction of light to see into awkward spots—like when a dentist looks at your back teeth!

If you shine a flashlight into a mirror, you can see how the mirror reflects the beam of light.

DISCOVER IT YOURSELF!

Find one or two small mirrors and try these different ways of reflecting light.

1. Can you read the numbers? You could practice mirror writing and send secret messages to your friends.

2. See around corners.

3. Make kaleidoscope patterns. (Place a mirror on each line.)

DISCOVER IT YOURSELF!

Make a periscope to look over the heads of a crowd of people or to peep over a wall.

1. Ask an adult to cut out two holes of the same size at the top and bottom of an empty juice or milk carton. One hole must be on each side.

2. Measure and draw two squares on both sides of each hole and divide the squares with diagonal lines. This is to help you make sure that the mirrors are at the same angle of 45°. Ask an adult to help.

3. Cut out two diagonal slits on each side, as shown. They should be just big enough to slide your mirrors through.

4. Slip the mirrors in place with the reflecting sides facing each other.

The picture to the right shows how the mirrors change the direction of light. Light hits the top mirror and is reflected down to the bottom mirror and then into your eyes.

Amazing Mirrors

Many mirrors are flat, but some are curved. A concave mirror curves down in the middle. If you stand close to a concave mirror, it magnifies you, so you look bigger. If you stand farther away, your reflection will be upside down. A convex mirror curves up in the middle. It makes you look smaller, but you can see more behind.

Convex

Concave

Curved mirrors can be fun! They reflect the light in different directions, so your reflection can look stretched, squashed, or twisted.

Look at your reflection in a bright, shiny spoon. In the convex side, you look smaller, but you can see a lot of the room behind you. In the concave side, your image will be big if you hold the spoon close but smaller and upside down if you hold it farther away.

Mirror

Bending Light

DISCOVER IT YOURSELF!

Test refraction with this magic coin trick. You will need a glass, a coin, a pencil, and some water.

1. Put a coin in the bottom of an empty glass. Look down into the glass and, at the same time, lower the pencil along the side until you think it is at the same height as the coin. Were you right?

2. Now fill the glass with water and try the experiment again. You will probably find that you do not lower your pencil far enough. This is because refraction makes the water look shallower than it really is.

A straight straw in a glass of water looks bent. This is because light travels more slowly through water than it does through air, and when light slows down, it can also change direction. This is called refraction. Glass refracts light, too. Look at some stamps through the bottom of a thick glass and see how their shapes change.

Light rays are refracted, or bent, as they pass from the water to the air, so the coin appears higher in the glass than it really is.

1

2

25

How Lenses Work

Lenses are pieces of glass or clear plastic that are specially curved to bend light by refraction. If you look through a concave lens, things look smaller. Convex lenses can make things look bigger. Magnifying glasses and microscopes have convex lenses. The lenses in eyeglasses help people see more clearly. We say that people who wear glasses with concave lenses are nearsighted, and people who wear glasses with convex lenses are farsighted.

Eye Spy

Do you or your friend wear glasses? Are the glasses concave or convex? The box on the next page tells you how to test them.

DISCOVER IT YOURSELF!

Make a simple magnifier to make things look bigger.

1. Cut a hole in a piece of cardboard or use a slide mount.

2. Cover the hole with clear plastic tape and use a pencil to drip a single drop of water over it. The rounded droplet should magnify things slightly.

You could also try looking at things through the bottom of a thick glass or a glass filled with water.

26

Testing Lenses

Collect some old pairs of glasses. First, look at some print in a book. If the words look smaller, the lenses are concave. If they look bigger, the lenses are convex. Another test for lenses is to look at the shadows they cast on a sheet of paper. Concave lenses spread the light, so they cast a big, dark shadow. Convex lenses concentrate the light. Their shadow is small and bright.

Convex lenses concentrate light

Concave lenses spread light

DISCOVER IT YOURSELF!

Try this experiment with a convex lens from an old pair of reading glasses or a magnifying glass to see how it concentrates light.

Stand with your back to a sunny window and hold up a sheet of white paper so that the light from the window is shining on it. Move your lens toward the paper until you can see an image of the window and the scene outside. The image will be upside down. The lenses in your eyes work in a similar way. Look at the box at the bottom of the next page.

How Do You See?

Look at your eyes in a mirror. The black spot in the middle is called the pupil. The colored part around the pupil is the iris. The size of the iris changes to make the pupil bigger or smaller. In very bright light, the pupil gets smaller so you are not dazzled. In dim light, the pupil gets larger to let more light into your eye. If you go into a dark room after being in strong sunlight, you can't see much at first. But after a while your eyes adjust and you can see more clearly.

Looking at Eyes

Look at your eyes in a mirror. Close them. Count to 20. Open your eyes. Your pupils will be larger to let in more light.

How Eyes Work

The lens collects the light that enters your eye and focuses a small picture onto the retina at the back of your eye. (This works in a similar way to the lens you used in the activity on page 27.) The retina sends messages about the picture to your brain. The brain sorts out the image so it looks the right way up, and you can make sense of what you see.

Retina

Optic nerve

Lens

Pupil

Seeing in the Dark

Owls and cats hunt for food at night. Owls have large pupils to collect as much light as possible.

During the day, a cat's pupils are narrow slits, but at night they become wider to let in more light.

Seeing All Around

A fly has large, dome-shaped eyes. Each eye is made up of thousands of tiny lenses, and no two lenses point in the same direction. A fly can therefore see danger coming from most directions—it's almost impossible to sneak up on a fly!

Eye Spy

Some people are color blind. This means that they cannot tell the difference between different colors. For example, someone who cannot tell the difference between red and green may not be able to see the correct numbers in the circles on the right. People with normal sight read the top number as 5 and the bottom one as 8. Those with red-green color blindness may read the numbers as 2 and 3. A few people are completely color blind. They see everything in only black, white, and gray.

29

Light of Many Colors

Sunlight is made up of different colors. You can sometimes see these colors when sunlight passes through glass or water. The glass or water bends the colors by different amounts, and this makes them spread out in a rainbow pattern which we call the spectrum. If it rains when the Sun is shining, the raindrops in the air sometimes separate the colors of sunlight and you see a rainbow in the sky.

Rainbow Colors

A rainbow has all the colors of the spectrum—red, orange, yellow, green, blue, indigo, and violet.

DISCOVER IT YOURSELF!

Here are some different ways of making your own rainbows.

Lay a mirror at an angle in a dish of water. Stand the dish in front of a sunny window so that the light travels into the water and is reflected from the mirror onto some cardboard. The water covering the mirror should split the sunlight into the colors of the spectrum.

Seeing Colors

Most things do not make light of their own. They reflect light. The colors we see depend on which colors are reflected into our eyes. So a red flower looks red because it reflects more of the red part of the spectrum into our eyes than the other colors.

Remember: never look directly at the Sun or a bright light.

Changing Colors

Look at the world through different colors. Shine a flashlight through colored candy wrappers, look through dyed water (food coloring works well), or buy colored light bulbs. These all filter light—a green filter only filters (lets through) green light.

31

Index